CONTEMPORARY ISSUES

GUN CONTROL

CONTEMPORARY ISSUES

CONTEMPORARY ISSUES

GUN CONTROL

JIM GALLAGHER

MASON CREST

PHILADELPHIA | MIAMI

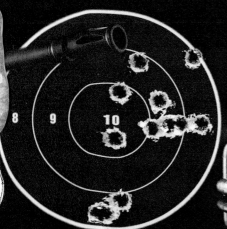

MASON CREST

450 Parkway Drive, Suite D, Broomall, Pennsylvania 19008
(866) MCP-BOOK (toll-free) • www.masoncrest.com

Printed and bound in the United States of America.

CPSIA Compliance Information: Batch #CCRI2019.
For further information, contact Mason Crest at 1-866-MCP-Book.

First printing
1 3 5 7 9 8 6 4 2

ISBN (hardback) 978-1-4222-4392-3
ISBN (series) 978-1-4222-4387-9
ISBN (ebook) 978-1-4222-7407-1

Library of Congress Cataloging-in-Publication Data
on file at the Library of Congress

Interior and cover design: Torque Advertising + Design
Production: Michelle Luke

Publisher's Note: Websites listed in this book were active at the time of publication. The publisher is not responsible for websites that have changed their address or discontinued operation since the date of publication. The publisher reviews and updates the websites each time the book is reprinted.

QR CODES AND LINKS TO THIRD-PARTY CONTENT

CONTENTS

KEY ICONS TO LOOK FOR:

 Words to Understand: These words with their easy-to-understand definitions will increase the reader's understanding of the text while building vocabulary skills.

 Sidebars: This boxed material within the main text allows readers to build knowledge, gain insights, explore possibilities, and broaden their perspectives by weaving together additional information to provide realistic and holistic perspectives.

 Educational videos: Readers can view videos by scanning our QR codes, providing them with additional educational content to supplement the text. Examples include news coverage, moments in history, speeches, iconic sports moments, and much more!

 Text-Dependent Questions: These questions send the reader back to the text for more careful attention to the evidence presented there.

 Research Projects: Readers are pointed toward areas of further inquiry connected to each chapter. Suggestions are provided for projects that encourage deeper research and analysis.

 Series Glossary of Key Terms: This back-of-the-book glossary contains terminology used throughout this series. Words found here increase the reader's ability to read and comprehend higher-level books and articles in this field.

WORDS TO UNDERSTAND

magazine—a ammunition storage chamber. It holds a supply of cartridges that can be loaded mechanically into the breech of a semi-automatic firearm.

organized crime—a term that refers to a complex network of criminals who work together in a systematic way to make money through illegal activity. The criminal organization is sometimes called a "crime family" or "mob."

sunset provision—a stipulation in legislation that a program be terminated at the end of an established period, unless it is formally renewed by lawmakers.

OVERVIEW AND HISTORY OF GUN CONTROL

Over 20,000 people were enjoying the music at the day-long Route 91 Harvest Festival in Las Vegas on October 1, 2017. At around 10 pm, country star Jason Aldean began singing his hit song "When She Says Baby." At first, some attendees though the "crack-crack" noises were fireworks going off to accompany the song. But as people in the crowd began to fall, the festival-goers realized that the noises were rapid-fire shots. Panicked, they ran and sought cover.

From a room on the thirty-second floor of the Mandalay Bay hotel across the street, a sixty-four-year-old man named Stephen Paddock fired into the festival crowd. Paddock had snuck twenty-four firearms into his hotel room. All but two of them were semiautomatic rifles, most of which had been legally modified by the addition of a "bump stock." The bump stock enables such rifles to fire rapidly like fully automatic military weapons. By pulling the trigger once and holding it down, Paddock could spray nine bullets per second into the screaming throng. Each of his weapons was equipped with a high-capacity **magazine** that held up to 100 rounds.

In less than ten minutes, Paddock was able to fire more than 1,100 bullets into the panicked crowd, killing fifty-eight people at the concert site. Another 850 people were

Pedestrians gather at a memorial for the victims of the 2017 Las Vegas mass shooting.

injured as they tried to flee from the carnage, including 422 who were hit with gunfire. By the time police could get to Paddock's hotel room, he had committed suicide.

The Las Vegas shooting is the deadliest mass shooting committed by an individual in the United States. Unfortunately, it is only one of many such shootings that have occurred in recent years. A year prior to the Las Vegas shooting, in June 2016, a former security guard named Omar Mateen murdered forty-nine people at a gay nightclub in Orlando, Florida. In November 2017, just a month after Paddock's spree, a man named Devin Patrick Kelley killed 26 people at the First Baptist Church in Sutherland Springs, Texas. And during the first six months of 2018, there were over two dozen school shootings, including mass shootings in Parkland, Florida (seventeen killed) and Santa Fe, Texas (ten killed).

Between 1966 and 2018, there have been over 150 incidents in which four or more people were killed by a lone shooter in a public place. "Public mass shootings account for a tiny fraction of the country's gun deaths, but they are uniquely terrifying because they occur without warning in the most mundane places," noted a *Washington Post* analysis. "Most of the victims are chosen not for what they have done but simply for where they happen to be."[4]

The increasing frequency of these attacks have angered and upset many Americans. However, Americans are deeply divided over the most effective response. Some believe that increased gun control is required, and advocate for new laws that would make it harder for people to buy guns. Others believe that existing laws, if properly enforced, are enough to prevent such shootings, and find it unfair to restrict the rights of millions of law-abiding gun owners.

Stoneman Douglas High School
-17 dead
-14 injured

0:00 | 0:00

To see how US presidents have responded to school shootings, scan here.

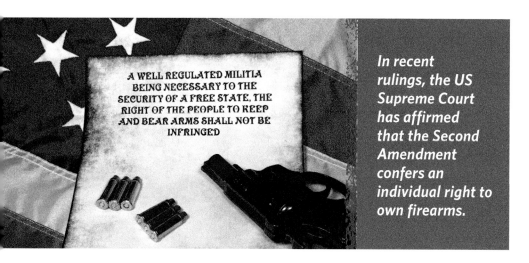

In recent rulings, the US Supreme Court has affirmed that the Second Amendment confers an individual right to own firearms.

A CHERISHED AMERICAN RIGHT

Historically, gun ownership has always held an important place in American culture. The Second Amendment to the US Constitution, ratified in 1791, reads, "A well regulated Militia, being necessary to the security of a free State, the right of the people to keep and bear Arms, shall not be infringed."[5]

For many Americans, a firearm is more than a tool for

"Strict gun control laws do not always have the effect that legislators intend. More guns (in the right hands) can stop crime, and fewer guns (in the wrong hands) can make for more crime. Gun control isn't crime control."[7]

—libertarian TV journalist John Stossel

For many Americans, hunting and sport shooting are an important part of their everyday lives. Participating in these outdoor activities teaches responsibility and respect for firearms.

hunting, target shooting, or personal protection. It's a symbol of self-reliance, and a critical defense against the threat of government tyranny. "The Second Amendment to the Constitution isn't for just protecting hunting rights, and it's not only to safeguard your right to target practice," noted US Senator Ted Cruz of Texas in a letter to supporters during his 2016 presidential campaign. "It is a Constitutional right to protect your children, your family, your home, our lives, and to serve as the ultimate check against governmental tyranny—for the protection of liberty."[6]

According to a 2017 study by the Pew Research Center, 72 percent of American gun owners possess a handgun. Most say that personal defense is their primary reason for owning a handgun. To be effective for this purpose, proper instruction in firing a handgun, as well as regular shooting practice, are required.

Data from government agencies such as the Bureau of Alcohol, Tobacco, Firearms, and Explosives (ATF) indicates that Americans possess more than 360 million firearms. That's an average of more than one gun per person (the US population was about 325 million in 2018). This represents a far higher gun ownership rate per capita than any other country in the world.

Of course, every person in the United States does not actually own a gun. A Pew Research Center study of gun ownership demographics, published in June 2017, found that 31 percent of Americans admitted that they currently owned a firearm. Another 11 percent said they did not own a gun personally, but lived with someone who did. Thus, the data indicates that at least 42 percent of American households contain firearms. Of the 69 percent of Americans who told Pew they did not currently own a gun, more than half said they could see themselves owning one at some time in the future.[7]

A PATCHWORK OF LAWS

Although Americans respect the right of gun ownership, more than two centuries of legal interpretation of the Constitution have indicated that this right is not absolute. For example, federal law prohibits certain categories of people—such as felons, the mentally ill, drug addicts, and illegal immigrants—from possessing firearms. Federal legislation also prohibits civilians from owning certain types of firearms, and regulates the sale and purchase of those weapons that are permitted.

Federal laws provide a basic framework for regulating the sale and possession of firearms, but individual states establish and control how residents can legally obtain, carry, and use firearms. Consequently, gun laws vary widely from state to state. Some states, such as New Jersey and New York, rarely issue permits allowing people to carry handguns. Other states, such as Alaska and Arizona, impose very few restrictions. Privileges that are taken for granted by gun owners in one state may become illegal once they cross the border into a neighboring state.

Sometimes, gun laws can vary within a state. Often, large cities will have stricter regulations on firearms than exist elsewhere in the state. For example, hunting is a way of life in rural Pennsylvania, and ownership of long guns (rifles and shotguns) for sporting use is relatively common throughout most of the state. However, the state's two major cities, Philadelphia and Pittsburgh, as well as some suburban municipalities, have imposed additional laws to restrict firearm ownership—particularly handguns, which they fear will be used to commit crimes.

Many gun rights activists bristle at firearms restrictions generally, but the lack of uniform laws across jurisdictions can be particularly upsetting to them. This situation, gun rights advocates argue, creates confusion and places an unfair burden on gun owners. Those who live in, or travel to, jurisdictions with the strictest firearms laws may even be deprived of their fundamental right to defend themselves, gun activists claim.

There is another side to the issue, however. Ensuring public safety is the most basic duty of any government. And when guns are used irresponsibly or criminally, innocent people may—and often do—suffer serious injury or death. So the question becomes, how should the individual's right to have a firearm be balanced with the

> *"Like most rights, the right secured by the Second Amendment is not unlimited. From Blackstone through the 19th-century cases, commentators and courts routinely explained that the right was not a right to keep and carry any weapon whatsoever in any manner whatsoever and for whatever purpose.... Nothing in our opinion should be taken to cast doubt on longstanding prohibitions on the possession of firearms by felons and the mentally ill, or laws forbidding the carrying of firearms in sensitive places such as schools and government buildings, or laws imposing conditions and qualifications on the commercial sale of arms."[2]*
>
> *—US Supreme Court Justice Antonin Scalia*

collective good of minimizing gun violence? Legislators and policy makers in different parts of the country have answered that question differently. The nation's current patchwork of gun laws is the result.

HISTORY OF GUN CONTROL

Until the early twentieth century, most gun laws in America encouraged gun ownership or expanded the pool of Americans who could own guns. In colonial America, most families owned at least one firearm, which was used for hunting and self-defense. In most colonies, the head of the household was required by law to own a gun.

The Militia Acts of 1792 did not apply to Black Americans, due to the fact that slavery was a fact of life in the United States. Southerners feared that slave insurrections would occur more regularly if blacks were allowed to own firearms. Throughout the South, state and local laws prohibited blacks from owning guns. These laws were often supported by the federal government. In the infamous 1857 case *Dred Scot v. Sanford*, the US Supreme Court ruled that black Americans could not enjoy the rights of American citizens. In his majority opinion, Chief Justice Roger B. Taney wrote that citizenship "would give to persons of the negro race, who were recognized as citizens in any one State of the Union, the right ... to keep and carry arms wherever they went."[8]

After the Civil War, a variety of federal laws were passed to protect the rights of newly freed blacks—including the right to keep and bear arms. Southern communities responded by passing laws that did not impose an outright ban on gun ownership based on race—as those could be struck down in federal courts as unconstitutional—but that made it nearly impossible for African Americans to own guns. For example, in 1871 the state legislature of Tennessee passed a law that made it illegal to buy inexpensive firearms other than certain military models. Most former confederate soldiers already owned the "Army and Navy guns," but the poor black freedmen could not afford them. Similar "Jim Crow" laws were enacted to prevent blacks from voting or challenging segregated systems.

In May 1792, a year after the Second Amendment to the Constitution was ratified, Congress passed a series of Militia Acts. At the time, the US only had a small standing army, so the legislation empowered the federal government to call on state or local militia forces in case of a national emergency. Under this legislation every every free, healthy white male citizen between the ages of eighteen and forty-five was required to own a firearm and bayonet, as well as a supply of gunpowder and ammunition.

By the 1930s, however, rising crime rates and the use of more powerful and deadly firearms led to the first federal laws that limited access to firearms. In general, these were a response to violent tactics used by a variety of gun-toting criminals.

Between 1920 and 1933, the sale of alcohol was banned in the United States. This period, called Prohibition, provided an opportunity for criminal gangs to get rich by smuggling alcohol into the country from Canada (where brewing and distilling were still legal) and selling it in underground nightclubs known as "speakeasies." In many American cities, ruthless gangsters like Lucky Luciano, Al Capone, and Vito Genovese fought for control of neighborhoods where they could distribute illicit booze. These turf wars were waged with weapons like the Thompson submachine gun, or "Tommy gun." Originally designed for military use, this rapid-fire, fully automatic rifle could be fitted with a fifty-round drum magazine.

"As underground profit margins surged, gang rivalries emerged, and criminal activity mounted. The homicide

Members of an Illinois gang during Prohibition, armed with rifles, revolvers, and Thompson submachine guns. The greater firepower that criminals could muster led Congress to pass gun-control laws during the 1930s.

rate across the nation rose 78 percent during Prohibition," writes Abigail Perkiss. "In Chicago alone, there were more than 400 gang-related murders a year. According to scholar Edward Sullivan, writing in 1929, Prohibition resulted in 'the greatest crime record ever attained by a nation.'"[9]

The Great Depression, which began in 1929, also contributed to the rise in crime and gun violence. The most infamous bank robbers of the era, such as John Dillinger, Clyde Barrow and Bonnie Parker, and Charles "Pretty Boy" Floyd, favored Tommy guns for their firepower. When local police tried to stop these robbers, they often found themselves hopelessly outgunned.

Congress responded to the rampant criminal violence by passing the nation's first major gun control legislation, the National Firearms Act of 1934. It targeted "gangster weapons"—submachine guns like the Tommy gun, as well as sawed-off shotguns and short-barreled rifles, which could easily be concealed under a coat. In the view of lawmakers, such weapons had no legitimate private use. The law didn't ban the weapons outright. Instead, it imposed a tax of $200 each time ownership of a covered weapon was transferred, and it required that the firearm be registered. The tax was very steep for the period—in 2018 dollars, an equivalent tax would be about $3,500. Violations were punishable by another heavy fine and up to five years in prison.

In 1938 Congress passed additional gun control measures in the Federal Firearms Act. It required firearms manufacturers and dealers involved in interstate or foreign commerce to pay an annual fee to obtain a federal license. It also required gun dealers to keep records of their sales. The act prohibited convicted felons, people under criminal indictment, and fugitives from justice from purchasing guns.

The next year, the US Supreme Court heard the case *United States v. Miller*, which challenged the National Firearms Act of 1934 as an unconstitutional infringement of the Second Amendment. The Court ruled unanimously against the arguments presented in *Miller*, finding no evidence that a sawed-off shotgun "has some reasonable relationship to the preservation or efficiency of a well

These New York police officers have drawn their guns during a 1960s race riot in Harlem. The 1960s were a time of social turmoil in the United States. An increase in the level of gun-related violence led American policy makers to call for new restrictions on gun ownership.

regulated militia," and thus "we cannot say that the Second Amendment guarantees the right to keep and bear such an instrument."[10]

CHANGING ATTITUDES

On November 22, 1963, a former US Marine named Lee Harvey Oswald assassinated President John F. Kennedy in Dallas. Oswald had purchased the Mannlicher-Carcano rifle used to kill the president through a magazine advertisement, and the weapon was mailed to a post-office box that he had rented under a fake name.

The assassination shocked the nation. Legislation was quickly introduced in the House of Representatives that would prevent the mail-order sale of rifles and shotguns. Other gun-control bills were also introduced in Congress. However, these bills were not approved, due in part to intense opposition from hunting and sportsmen's organizations.

Over the next five years, gun control legislation continued to be introduced in Congress. Politicians found themselves in a difficult position on the issue. Although most of their constituents might support gun control, a vocal, organized, and increasingly well-funded interest group—what would come to be called the "gun lobby"—opposed it. As a result, most members of Congress refused to take a position on the issue, and gun control legislation went nowhere.

Shocking events in 1967 and 1968 changed the situation. In July 1967 deadly race riots erupted in the cities of Detroit, Michigan, and Newark, New Jersey. In both cases, police and National Guard troops came under fire when they tried to stop the disturbances. In one neighborhood on Detroit's east side, armed rioters held the authorities at bay for three full days.

The Kerner Commission, formed to investigate the cause of the riots and offer suggestions for avoiding future incidents, issued a report in February 1968. The report noted that the high number of guns in circulation had helped ignite and sustain the riots—and would put other American cities at risk for large-scale civil unrest. The report's authors drew "the firm conclusion that effective firearms controls are an essential contribution to domestic peace and tranquility."[11]

Less than two months later, on April 4, 1968, a white supremacist used a hunting rifle to kill civil rights leader Martin Luther King Jr. in Memphis, Tennessee. The assassination touched off riots in more than 100 cities. Just like during the previous year's riots, police and National Guardsmen were shot at by armed rioters. And as the street violence was finally winding down, John F. Kennedy's younger brother Robert, a former US Attorney General and a candidate for the Democratic Party's presidential nomination in the 1968 election, was shot and killed in California on June 6 by a man who had illegally purchased a .22 caliber handgun.

By the end of 1968, two new pieces of legislation overhauled the nation's firearms laws.
The Omnibus Crime Control and Safe Streets Act made

the mail-order sale of handguns illegal and set a minimum age of twenty-one years for handgun purchases and eighteen years for long gun purchases. The Gun Control Act of 1968 banned interstate sales of all firearms, as well as the importation of surplus military weapons. It also required all gun dealers to obtain a federal firearms license (previously, the license was not required if the gun dealer did not engage in interstate sales.) The Gun Control Act also expanded the categories of people ineligible to purchase a firearm to include drug abusers and people with a mental disorder.

The next major firearms legislation addressed some concerns that had been raised by gun-rights advocates. The Firearms Owners Protection Act of 1986 eased restrictions on the sale and transfer of ammunition, lightened the paperwork requirements for gun dealers, and limited ATF inspections of paperwork to once a year. The new law also allowed licensed dealers to sell firearms at temporary events, or "gun shows," in their state. The law did include some gun-control provisions, making it illegal to own or sell new machine guns and silencers.

THE BRADY ACT

On March 30, 1981, a small crowd of people gathered outside a hotel in Washington, D.C., hoping to see President Ronald Reagan, who had given a speech inside. As Reagan left the hotel, a man in the crowd suddenly fired six shots from a .22 caliber revolver at Reagan and his entourage. The president was wounded, as were three others who accompanied him: Secret Service agent Timothy McCarthy, D.C. police officer Thomas Delahanty, and the president's press secretary, James Brady.

Shot in the head, Brady was not expected to survive. He did, although he suffered brain damage and was partially paralyzed. Brady and his wife, Sarah, became outspoken advocates for stricter firearms laws, particularly regarding handguns.

Moments after President Reagan was shot in 1981, he is surrounded by Secret Service agents (left). Reagan's press secretary James Brady (in blue business suit) and policeman Thomas Delahanty lie wounded on the sidewalk. Brady would become a powerful advocate for stricter laws regulating ownership of firearms, particularly handguns.

The assassination attempt exposed a problem with the existing US firearms regulations: the system relied on prospective gun buyers to be truthful. The assassin, twenty-five-year-old John Hinckley Jr., should not have been able to purchase a gun. Hinckley also had a history of psychiatric problems, and had previously been arrested for illegal possession of firearms. But he lied on the paperwork he submitted when he purchased the revolver from a Dallas pawnshop.

Lying on a firearms application was a felony. But clearly the possibility of future punishment would not deter everybody who was ineligible to own a gun, yet eager to acquire one. Sarah Brady led an effort to tighten the rules for gun purchases, and James Brady served as a powerful symbol for this cause.

In 1987, legislation dubbed the Brady Bill was introduced in Congress. It called for a mandatory background check, to be performed by law enforcement, for everyone who sought to buy a handgun from a federally licensed dealer. Conducting such background checks would take time, so the Brady Bill set a seven-day waiting period between a prospective buyer's application and his or her actual receipt of the weapon.

Gun rights advocates were unhappy about the waiting period, and they opposed the Brady Bill. The National Rifle Association and other pro-gun groups spent millions of dollars lobbying against the legislation. Although the original bill did not pass in the 100th Congress, it was reintroduced in 1989, 1991, and 1993, when it was finally passed by the 103rd Congress. It was signed into law by President Bill Clinton on November 30, 1993.

The Brady Handgun Violence Prevention Act was similar to the original Brady Bill, albeit with some compromises intended to gain support from gun rights advocates. The waiting period for handgun purchases was reduced from seven to five days. More important, the law required that waiting periods eventually be eliminated by a system for instant background checks. As required by the law, the National Instant Criminal Background Check System (NICS) went online in 1998.

ADDITIONAL LEGISLATION

A year after passage of the Brady Act, President Clinton signed the Violent Crime Control and Law Enforcement Act. This legislation made it illegal to "manufacture, transfer, or possess a semiautomatic assault weapon," unless it was "lawfully possessed under Federal law on the date of the enactment of this subsection" in September 1994. Nineteen military-style weapons, including the AR-15, TEC-9, and MAC-10 rifles, could not be manufactured or sold. The act also banned high-capacity magazines. However, the assault weapons ban included a sunset provision, meaning it would expire after ten years unless it was renewed by Congress. By September 2004, control of the White House and Congress had changed and the assault weapons ban was permitted to expire.

Other firearms-related legislation during the presidency

of George W. Bush (2001-2009) was more focused on protecting the rights of gun owners than on restricting gun ownership. In 2003, Congress attached a provision to the legislation that funded the Bureau of Alcohol, Tobacco, Firearms, and Explosives (ATF) known as the Tiahrt Amendment. The amendment prevents the ATF from publicly releasing information that shows where criminals purchased firearms. This amendment prevents experts who are researching gun use in crime from accessing this data, and it cannot be used in lawsuits against firearms dealers.

The Protection of Lawful Commerce in Arms Act, passed in 2005, protects gun manufacturers from being named in federal

The Tiahrt Amendment is named for former congressman Todd Tiahrt, who represented Kansas in the House of Representatives from 1995 until 2011. During his career in Congress, Tiahrt received an A+ rating from the National Rifle Association for his support of pro-gun legislation.

or state civil lawsuits by those who were victims of crimes involving guns made by that company.

Two major decisions by the US Supreme Court will undoubtedly influence future legislation. In *District of Columbia v. Heller* (2008), the Court ruled that residents of Washington, D.C., could possess handguns in their homes, and could transport them for a "lawful recreational purpose," such as using the gun at a shooting range. This overturned a longtime ban on handgun ownership in the federal district. Another case, *McDonald v. City of Chicago* (2010), affirmed the precedent in *Heller* that the Constitution prevents federal, state, or local governments from completely banning firearms (particularly handguns).

US Supreme Court in Washington, DC

TEXT-DEPENDENT QUESTIONS

1. What right does the Second Amendment to the US Constitution protect?
2. What percentage of Americans own a firearm, according to the Pew Research Center?
3. Why was the National Firearms Act of 1934 passed by Congress?
4. Who was James Brady?

 RESEARCH PROJECTS

Over the past 40 years, the intent of the Second Amendment has been hotly disputed, due in part to its wording. Some people believe the amendment was meant to empower state militias, not permit all private citizens to own firearms. Read the amendment, then go online and examine both sides of the issue. Then write a report about how you interpret the amendment, explaining and justifying your decision.

2nd Amendment

hollow-point bullets—a bullet that is designed with an indentation at its tip. When the bullet strikes a target, this design causes this bullet to expand, causing greater damage as it penetrates the target.

red flag—a warning of danger or a potential problem.

white supremacist—a person who believes that the white race is inherently better than other races.

SHOULD ADDITIONAL GUN CONTROL LAWS BE ENACTED?

CHAPTER 2

Dylan Roof should not have been able to purchase a gun from a federally licensed firearms dealer. He had been arrested in February 2015 after acting suspiciously at a shopping mall in Columbia, South Carolina. Police who searched him found illegal drugs. When he returned to the mall he was arrested and charged with trespassing. In early March 2015, Roof was arrested a second time, this time for drug possession, a felony.

In mid-April 2015, about a week after his twenty-first birthday, Roof went into a South Carolina gun store called Shooter's Choice. He picked out a .45 caliber Glock handgun that he liked, and filled out Form 4473, a document that federal laws require to purchase a firearm. There is a three-day waiting period to purchase a handgun, during which time a background check is performed.

Roof's previous arrests, particularly felony drug charges, should have thrown up a **red flag**. Under federal guidelines for the National Instant Criminal Background Check System (NICS), Roof's application should have immediately been denied. However, a clerk at the prison where Roof had been detained in March 2015 had made a mistake on the police report submitted to the NICS, attributing the arrest to the Lexington County Sheriff's

Department, not the Columbia Police Department. When the NICS contacted the sheriff's department as part of Roof's background check, it did not find a report about his drug arrest because that report had been filed by the city police, not the county.

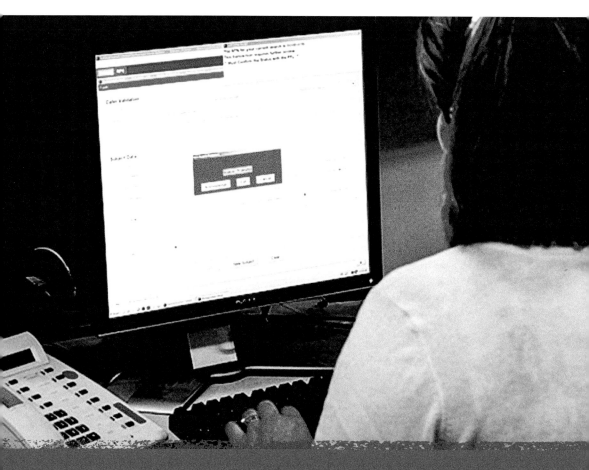

A NICS examiner reviews background information to determine whether an applicant is eligible to purchase a firearm. The National Instant Criminal Background Check System, or NICS, is a provision of the 1993 Brady Act that requires background checks on individuals purchasing firearms or receiving them through some other means. The NICS Section is located at the FBI's Criminal Justice Information Services Division in Clarksburg, West Virginia.

Due to confusion involving the two law-enforcement agencies, the store had not yet received a response from NICS when Roof returned to Shooter's Choice three days later. Without a formal denial from federal officials, firearms dealers can legally complete sales to customers once the three-day waiting period expires. Roof purchased the Glock handgun, using cash his father had given to him for his birthday. The handgun came with three magazines, each capable of holding 13 rounds, and Roof purchased five additional magazines.

On the evening of June 17, 2015, Roof carried his handgun into a bible study class at the historic Emanuel AME Church in downtown Charleston. He fired over seventy **hollow-point bullets** at the people in the class, killing nine of them and wounding another. Roof, a **white supremacist**, was motivated by racial hatred of the largely black congregation, and admitted after his arrest that he had hoped the mass shooting would start a race war.

Afterward, both sides of the gun-control debate attempted to use the Dylan Roof case to bolster their own arguments. US Senator Charles E. Grassley, the chairman of the Senate Judiciary Committee and a gun-rights supporter, commented on the fact that the NICS should have blocked Roof's purchase of a firearm. "It's disastrous that this bureaucratic mistake prevented existing laws from working and blocking an illegal gun sale," Grassley said in a statement. "The facts undercut attempts to use the tragedy to enact unnecessary gun laws. The American people, and especially the victims' families, deserve better."[14]

On the other hand, the Center for American Progress, a liberal-leaning public policy organization, said that the case showed that the background check system needed to be improved. "Like the Virginia Tech massacre, the Columbine massacre, and countless every day shootings, gaps in our gun background check system contributed to the Charleston attack," Arkadi Gerney, a senior vice president at the center, said in a statement. "The answer is simple: all records of prohibited individuals need to go in the FBI system and every gun sale needs to go through a background check."[15]

HOW THE NICS WORKS

Background checks for firearms purchases were mandated by the Brady Handgun Violence Prevention Act of 1993. The current NICS system was launched by the FBI in 1998. Its purpose is to determine whether a prospective buyer is eligible to purchase firearms. Over the past twenty years, the NICS has processed more than 230 million background checks, and denied more than 1.3 million purchases by ineligible buyers.

The system works like this: when a person wants to buy a firearm from a federally licensed dealer, they must fill out Form 4473. The clerk then contacts the NICS system, which is located at an FBI facility in West Virginia. The contact can be by phone or via a computer system called E-check. The NICS cross-checks the prospective buyer's information against three FBI databases that contain criminal reports. If the prospective buyer does not appear in any of these databases, the sale can proceed. In such cases the background check is often completed in less than fifteen minutes. However, if the buyer does appear on one of the databases, then a worker at the NICS must do further investigation to determine whether or not the person is eligible or ineligible to purchase a firearm. The Brady Act allows the FBI three business days to complete this investigation and either approve or deny the sale. If the firearms dealer has not received the FBI's decision at the end of that three-day period, it is permitted to complete the sale.

The current background check system is not perfect, as the Dylan Roof case showed. A similar problem with the NICS database was uncovered after another mass shooting at a church, this one in Sutherland Springs, Texas. The gunman, twenty-six-year-old Devin Patrick Kelley, killed twenty-six people and injured twenty others. A subsequent investigation found that Kelley should not have been able to purchase a weapon, because he had been charged with domestic violence while in the US Air Force and convicted in a court martial. However, the Air Force had accidentally failed to record Kelley's conviction in the appropriate FBI database, and it did not come up when his background check was conducted.

"Legislation that reduces the easy availability and number of firearms is the best way to respond to mass school shootings, church shootings, domestic violence and firearm-suicide."[12]

—Devin Hughes, the founder of GVPedia, and Mark Bryant, executive director of the Gun Violence Archive

National opinions on gun control have changed over time. In March 2018, the Gallup Organization found that 67 percent of Americans felt that the laws covering the sale of firearms should be made more strict than they are now, while 28 percent felt they should be kept the same and 4 percent said the laws should be less strict. The percentage of Americans supporting more gun control has risen steadily since 2010, when 44 percent felt the laws should be more strict, 42 percent felt they should be kept the same, and 12 percent felt they should be less strict.[16] The short essays that follow examine both sides of this issue.

ADDITIONAL GUN CONTROL LAWS ARE NEEDED

Many gun-control supporters believe that universal background checks represent a critical first step toward reducing gun violence in the United States. The Brady Act requires federally licensed firearms dealers to conduct background checks and submit records of all gun sales to the government. However, when a private individual sells

In many states, private individuals are allowed to sell firearms without a background check at gun shows, so long as selling guns is not their primary occupation. This "gun show loophole" concerns those who feel the lack of oversight opens the way for criminals or the mentally ill to procure firearms.

a firearm, he or she is not required by federal law to submit the purchaser's information to NICS for a background check. The seller does not have to impose a waiting period, or submit any record of the transfer to federal authorities, as long as the sale does not cross state lines and does not include a prohibited weapon (such as a submachine gun or short-barrel shotgun).

The media often refers to this practice as the "gun show loophole," because some of these unlicensed sales take place at gun shows. However, the same rules apply to any private firearms transaction, no matter where it takes place—a gun show, a flea market, between family members or neighbors, or over the Internet.

No one is certain about how many legal firearms transactions occur without a background check. A figure of 40 percent is often cited, but that is based on data from the early 1990s and probably is no longer accurate. A study published in 2017 by researchers from the School of Public Health at Harvard University found that about 22 percent of gun owners did not undergo a background check when they obtained their most recent firearm.[17]

"When unlicensed sellers don't run background checks, people known to be dangerous can easily obtain guns, often with deadly consequences," notes the Giffords Law Center to Prevent Gun Violence. "For example, in 2012, a gunman killed three people, including his wife, and injured four others at a spa in Wisconsin, after buying a gun through a private seller he found online. The shooter was prohibited from purchasing guns due to an active domestic

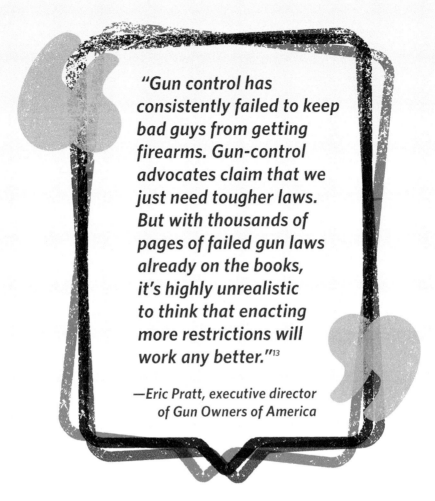

"Gun control has consistently failed to keep bad guys from getting firearms. Gun-control advocates claim that we just need tougher laws. But with thousands of pages of failed gun laws already on the books, it's highly unrealistic to think that enacting more restrictions will work any better."[13]

—Eric Pratt, executive director of Gun Owners of America

violence restraining order against him, but was able to buy the gun anyway because the seller was not required to run a background check.[18]

Currently, several states have taken steps to close the "gun show loophole." Ten states (California, Colorado, Connecticut, Delaware, Nevada, New York, Oregon, Rhode Island, Vermont, and Washington) and the District of Columbia require background checks at the point of sale for all firearms sales and transfers. Maryland and Pennsylvania require background checks for all handgun sales, but not for the sale of rifles or shotguns. Hawaii,

Illinois, Massachusetts, and New Jersey require prospective gun purchasers to acquire a permit, which includes a background check, before they can purchase any firearm. Iowa, Michigan, Nebraska, and North Carolina have a permit and background check requirement for the purchase of handguns, but not long guns.

One way to completely close the loophole would be a federal law that would require a permit to purchase any firearm, including those sold at gun shows and through private sales between individuals. One proposed form of the "permit-to-purchase" (PTP) program would require prospective gun purchasers to apply for the permit in person at a local law-enforcement office, have their

The AR-15 is one of the most popular semi-automatic rifles available in the United States.

fingerprints taken, and submit a photograph along with their paperwork. The permit-seeker would also be subject to a background check. Once the permit is approved, it would be good for five years. As long as the permit holder did not get in trouble with the law during that period, he or she would not have to undergo other background checks to purchase additional firearms.

The effectiveness of PTP laws can be seen in their absence. The state of Missouri once had a strong PTP law. After the law was repealed in 2007, researchers from Johns Hopkins University found that the rate of murders committed by firearms increased by 14 percent and firearm-related suicides increased by 16 percent. "After controlling for changes in crime, incarceration, police, poverty, and unemployment as well as other key laws, the repeal of Missouri's PTP law was associated with an increase of 1 homicide per every 100,000 population per year through 2012, translating to about 55 to 60 additional homicides per year," wrote Daniel W. Webster, Jon S. Vernick, Emma E. McGinty, and Ted Alcorn. "The increase occurred only for homicides committed with firearms and was observed in each of the most populous counties in the state, but it did not occur in any of the eight states bordering Missouri."[19]

Another way to keep guns out of the hands of those who should not have them would be to improve the data that states report to federal databases accessed by the NICS. Although federal law prohibits the sale of firearms to individuals with mental illness, the law currently does not require states to submit mental health information to the NICS. As a result, some people known to have several mental illnesses have passed background checks and obtained firearms. Standardizing the data that states submit to the federal government, and shortening the reporting period, should help to prevent this problem.

Data is critical to understanding the issue of gun

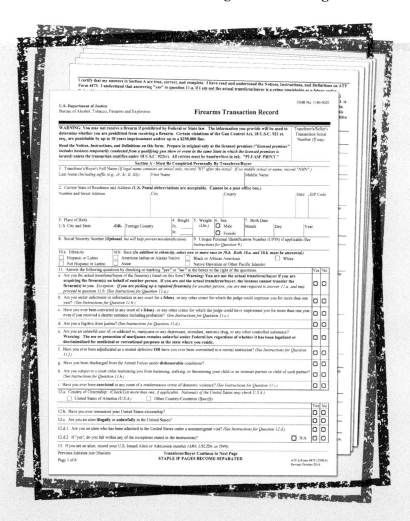

A firearms transaction record, or Form 4473, must be filled out to purchase any firearm from a federally licensed dealer.

violence—so it makes sense that the government should study the issue and provide non-biased information for policymakers. Yet although many experts—including the American Medical Association (AMA) and the American Public Health Association—have called gun violence a public health crisis, government agencies like the Centers for Disease Control and the National Institutes of Health have stopped conducting studies on the issue over the past two decades. This is due to a provision in a federal appropriations bill from 1996, which stated, "none of the funds made available for injury prevention and control at the Centers for Disease Control and Prevention may be used to advocate or promote gun control."[20]

The Centers for Disease Control is best known for fighting diseases, but it has other important public-health responsibilities. The CDC studies drownings, accidental falls, traumatic brain injuries, car crashes, suicides, and more. And although mass shootings attract media attention, they account for only a small fraction of the 30,000 annual gun deaths in the United States. More than half of these deaths are suicides. Yet since 1996 the CDC and other agencies have not been able to focus on gun ownership as a risk factor for suicides.

Another step would be re-imposing a ban on so-called "assault weapons," similar to the one that existed from 1994 to 2004. The original assault weapons provision of the law prohibited the sale of certain semi-automatic rifles, such as the popular AR-15 rifle, as well as large-capacity magazines for rifles and handguns.

Scan here to view a news report on the AR-15 rifle.

The AR-15 shoots relatively small rounds (.223 caliber), but the high velocity causes them to shatter once they penetrate the target's body. The damage this causes within the body is much more devastating than the effects of higher-caliber, but lower velocity, bullets fired from a handgun. Semi-automatic rifles can also be equipped with magazines that hold thirty round or more, allowing a shooter to fire more shots before having to reload. Most of the deadliest mass shootings—including Sandy Hook in 2012, Las Vegas in 2017, and Parkland in 2018—were carried out by madmen bearing AR-15 rifles. Many gun-control advocates believe that banning these weapons would be a step in the right direction.

Ultimately, members of Congress will have to fight off the influence of well-funded organizations that advocate for gun rights, such as the National Rifle Association, if they are to implement tighter controls on the private sale and use of firearms.

ADDITIONAL GUN CONTROL LAWS ARE NOT NEEDED

The phrase "common-sense gun laws" is often invoked by politicians, the media, and gun-control advocates, especially after a mass shooting. While that term sounds great, most gun advocates agree that, with a deeper inspection of the facts, many "common sense" proposals would have little to no effect on gun crime. Their primary effect would be to impose additional restrictions and inconveniences on law-abiding citizens who wish to keep and bear arms.

For example, supporters of gun control often demand that Congress re-impose the federal ban on so-called "assault weapons," which existed from 1994 to 2004. However, most crimes involving firearms are committed with handguns, rather than rifles. According to data from the FBI, approximately 65 to 70 percent of firearms-related homicide cases each year involve handguns, while rifles were used in just 3 percent. (The type of gun used is not specified in about 28 percent of cases.) Thus a new assault weapons ban would have little effect on gun-related crime in the United States. "There is little theoretical basis to suggest that bans of assault weapons and high-capacity magazines would impact rates of suicide or unintentional injury," noted an analysis from the RAND Corporation.[21] "And although these policies could plausibly impact defensive gun use, the magnitudes of any such effects

In 2017 New York Congresswoman Carolyn Maloney introduced legislation in the House of Representatives that would require a background check for all firearms sales at gun shows.

are likely small. The FBI reported that, in 2015, eight of the 328 firearm-related justifiable homicides by private citizens involved any type of rifle."

In fact, it is likely that any new assault weapons ban would not apply to millions of semi-automatic rifles that were sold prior to the legislation's passage. For example, after the Parkland school shooting, Democrats in the US House of Representatives introduced a bill called the Assault Weapons Ban of 2018. It failed to advance in the Republican-controlled Congress, but if the legislation had passed it would have only prevented the sale of new firearms. Under this bill, as well as other similar legislative proposals, those who already legally owned semi-automatic rifles or high-capacity magazines would still be permitted to keep and use them.

This was also the case with the original 1994 assault weapons ban. However, the number of such weapons is much higher now than it was then. No one is certain exactly how many AR-15 rifles and similar weapons are out there, because the federal government is prevented by law from registering gun owners or firearms transactions. However, according to the National Rifle Association, there are between 8.5 million and 15 million semi-automatic rifles in the United States today, based on manufacturer data.[22] With so many guns in circulation, a person who intended to use an AR-15 illegally could probably still get one despite the federal ban.

Another often proposed "common sense" reform is closing the "gun show loophole" by requiring a background check for private firearms sales, whether they are transacted at a gun show or elsewhere. However, under federal law it's already illegal for a convicted felon to handle or purchase a weapon at a gun show. Those who do are subject to ten years in prison. It is similarly illegal for drug addicts, fugitives from justice, those who have committed domestic violence, or the mentally ill to attempt to purchase any type of gun. Straw purchases— where a person buys a gun on behalf of someone else who is in a prohibited category—are also illegal.

"What is the real point of closing the so-called "gun show loophole," asks Mark Keefe in an essay published in *American Rifleman*, the magazine of the NRA. "If it is to prohibit criminals from obtaining firearms, all the tools are already there. Bottom line, if it's illegal under federal law, it's illegal at a gun show. How about enforcing the law? ... Federal and state laws regarding firearms apply to every corner of the nation—including gun shows."[23]

Statistics published by the US Department of Justice

According to a Gallup Organization opinion poll from October 2017, 96 percent of Americans support background checks for all firearms purchases.

in 2002 found that less than 1 percent of those convicted of gun-related crimes had purchased their weapons at a gun show. Nearly 40 percent had purchased them from illegal street dealers.[24] A more recent study, published in 2016, examined over 760 firearms that had been taken from criminals by Pittsburgh police. According to that study, 79 percent of guns had been in the possession of people who were prohibited from owning firearms under current laws. At least 30 percent of the weapons had previously been reported as stolen.[25] Enforcing the existing laws would do much more to reduce crime than would placing additional restrictions on law-abiding gun owners.

TEXT-DEPENDENT QUESTIONS

1. Why should Dylan Roof's application to purchase a handgun have been denied?
2. When did the National Instant Criminal Background Check System go online?
3. How many semi-automatic rifles like the popular AR-15 do Americans currently own?

 ## RESEARCH PROJECTS

Laws that require background checks before firearms purchases have been a controversial issue in American politics. Investigate the positions of leading Democrats and leading Republicans. Which side do you agree with? Do you think both sides have valid points? Write a one-page essay on what you think Congress should do about this issue. Support your opinions by citing relevant evidence.

WORDS TO UNDERSTAND

barricade—an improvised barrier that is intended to delay an attacker.

corroborate—to confirm or support.

model—a system developed by analyzing data, presented as a mathematical description of a state of affairs.

CAN TOUGHER LAWS PREVENT SCHOOL AND MASS SHOOTINGS?

CHAPTER 3

At around 2:20 PM on February 14, 2018, a nineteen-year-old named Nikolas Cruz walked into a school building on the campus of Marjory Stoneman Douglas High School in Parkland, Florida. Cruz was carrying a soft black case that held an AR-15 rifle, along with multiple magazines. He pulled a fire alarm, then began walking through the school and shooting at the people within. Students took cover under desks, and teachers **barricaded** their classrooms.

The shooting lasted less than ten minutes. When it was over, fourteen students and three teachers had been killed, and seventeen others were wounded. It was one of the deadliest school shootings in US history.

In the wake of the Parkland shooting, many Americans called for stricter laws to regulate gun ownership. A group of Stoneman Douglas students who survived the shooting formed a group called Never Again MSD, which encouraged rallies and walk-outs at schools to protest gun violence, as well as a march in Washington, D.C. That event on March 24, 2018, called the March for Our Lives, drew more than 1.2 million protesters asking for stricter gun laws. At many schools, student walkouts occurred for seventeen minutes, in honor of the seventeen people killed in Parkland.

Scan here to watch Marjory Stoneman Douglas High School student David Hogg speak at the 2018 March for Our Lives in Washington, D.C.

In the wake of the shooting, Florida's legislature passed several gun-control measures. The new state law raised the minimum age for buying a rifle from eighteen to twenty-one and established waiting periods and background checks for gun purchases. It also included provisions for hiring police officers to serve in schools, and for allowing teachers that were properly trained to carry firearms. Other states debated similar measures.

The brief essays that follow examine whether or not tougher laws can prevent school or mass shootings.

TOUGHER LAWS CAN PREVENT SCHOOL AND MASS SHOOTING

No law can eliminate the risk of a mass shooting, as these are highly unpredictable events. However, many experts believe that implementing tougher laws—in particular,

The mass shooting at Marjory Stoneman Douglas High School in Parkland, Florida, led to a national outpouring of grief, as well as student-led protests for gun control.

imposing new bans on high-capacity magazines and on semi-automatic rifles that are considered assault weapons—would go a long way toward reducing the frequency of mass shootings, as well as the number of people killed in these tragic events.

In 2016, Louis Klarevas, a professor at the University of Massachusetts, published the book *Rampage Nation*, which revealed the results of his research into gun massacres over a thirty-year period. Klarevas defined "gun massacres" as high-fatality mass shootings in which six or more people die. During the ten-year period from 1984 to 1994, before the original assault weapons ban was passed by Congress, Klarevas found there were 19 gun massacres, which killed 155 people. During the period covered by the federal ban

A March for Our Lives rally in Orlando, 2018.

> *"My generation—having spent our entire lives seeing mass shooting after mass shooting—has learned that our voices are powerful and our votes matter. We must educate ourselves and start conversations that keep our country moving forward and we will. We hereby promise to fix the broken system we've been forced into and create a better world for the generations to come."*[26]
>
> *—Cameron Kasky, a survivor of the shooting at Marjory Stoneman Douglas High School in Parkland, Florida*

on assault weapons (1994-2004), the number of massacres dropped to 12 and the number killed fell to 89. But in the decade after the ban was allowed to expire (2004-2014), the number of massacres rose to 34, with 302 killed.[28]

"The original intent of the assault weapons ban was to reduce the carnage of mass shootings," Klarevas told the *Washington Post* shortly after the Parkland shooting. "And on that front the data indicate that it worked. ... In the last three years we have had as many gun massacres with assault weapons as in the decade prior. The trend is continuing to escalate."[29]

Despite prohibitions on federal funding for research into the causes of gun violence, there have been numerous studies that seem to **corroborate** Klarevas's findings. A review of all the scientific studies conducted between 1970 and 2016, published in the *Journal of the American Medical Association*, concluded that stronger background checks and permit-to-purchase laws tended to reduce firearm homicide rates.

Permit-to-purchase laws are considered to be among the most effective solutions because they involve local law enforcement officers in the decision about who gets a gun. The Parkland school shooter, Nikolas Cruz, was known in the community for being violent and dangerous. School officials would not allow him to carry a backpack on the campus. But before the Florida gun laws were tightened, Cruz or someone like him could walk into a gun store and legally purchase an AR-15 rifle, because he had not yet committed a felony that would appear in a NICS background check. Local police were aware of Cruz's history of violent outbursts and his reputation, and it's highly unlikely they would ever have approved a permit for him to purchase a weapon—especially one as potentially deadly as a semi-automatic rifle.

"In reality, the best research shows what common sense tells us: More guns mean more crime and more death," write gun violence researchers Devin Hughes and Mark Bryant. "Gun possession significantly increases your risk of being killed by someone you know. A gun in the home doubles your risk of homicide and triples your risk of suicide. The presence of a gun increases the lethality of domestic violence. Areas with higher gun ownership see

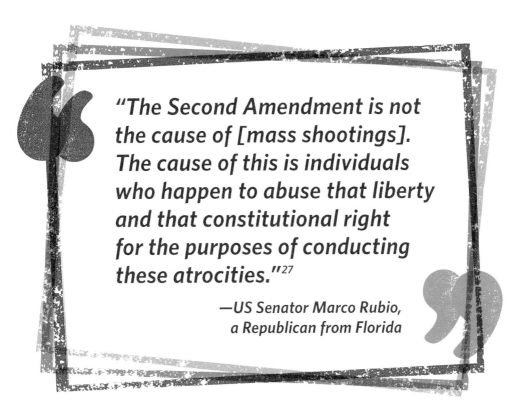

"The Second Amendment is not the cause of [mass shootings]. The cause of this is individuals who happen to abuse that liberty and that constitutional right for the purposes of conducting these atrocities."[27]

—US Senator Marco Rubio,
a Republican from Florida

a significant increase in burglary. And states with higher levels of gun ownership experience higher rates of firearm fatalities."[30]

Opinion surveys indicate that many American teachers agree with certain gun-control proposals as a way to make schools safer. In a 2018 survey by the Gallup Organization, teachers were given a list of nineteen proposals, ranging from "Limit exposure to violent entertainment," to "Arm staff, teachers," and asked to select the ones most likely to prevent school shootings. The teachers were allowed to choose more than one proposal. Gallup found that 33 percent of the teachers supported stricter gun laws, 22 percent endorsed a ban of assault weapons, and 10 percent wanted stricter background checks on firearms purchases.

Nineteen percent supported increased funding for better mental health care, while 15 percent wanted greater security at schools, such as bulletproof doors and windows or armed guards.[31]

TOUGHER LAWS WON'T PREVENT SCHOOL AND MASS SHOOTING

In May 2018, a seventeen-year-old named Dimitrios Pagourtzis killed nine students and a teacher in a mass shooting at Santa Fe High School near Houston, Texas. The shooting was a tragedy—but it could have been much worse. In the months and years before the attack occurred, the Santa Fe School District had done nearly everything it could to prevent such an event. The district had developed an award-winning, thorough plan for dealing with an active shooter on campus. The school conducted regular drills for teachers and students, including one just a few weeks before the rampage. Two armed and well-trained police officers patrolled the school campus each day, interacting with students while also providing security. The two officers were able to subdue Pagourtzis and end the shooting, despite one of them being seriously injured by a shotgun blast.

The local sheriff and school district administrators credited the officers' brave response with saving many lives. They also noted that, despite all their precautions, there is no guaranteed way to ensure that mass shootings can't happen. "My first indication is that our policies and procedures worked," commented J.R. "Rusty" Norman,

Seung-Hui Cho, a South Korean immigrant to the United States, had a long history of mental and emotional problems. His strange, and sometimes aggressive, behavior disturbed and alarmed teachers and classmates at Virginia Polytechnic Institute and State University. However, Cho had no history of actual violence until April 16, 2007, when he committed the deadliest school shooting in US history.

Cho passed two background checks, and was able to legally purchase a pair of semiautomatic handguns in February and March of 2007. Early on the morning of April 16, he murdered two students in a dormitory. Cho then changed his clothes and went to Norris Hall, a four-story academic building on the Virginia Tech campus. After getting inside around 9:15 am, he chained shut the three main entrances to the building. Then he began working his way through the building, shooting teachers and students. Cho's rampage ended at around 9:50 am; he committed suicide when police finally forced their way into the building. Before taking his own life, Cho had killed 32 people and wounded seventeen others.

In a rambling, incoherent video that he mailed to NBC News the morning of the shooting, Cho compared himself to the Columbine killers Eric Harris and Dylan Klebold. He also blamed others for his actions. "You had 100 billion chances and ways to avoid today," he ranted. "But you decided to spill my blood. You forced me into a corner and gave me only one option. The decision was yours. Now you have blood on your hands that will never wash off."[33]

president of the school district's board of trustees, shortly after the shooting. "Having said that, the way things are, if someone wants to get into a school to create havoc, they can do it."[32]

Often, one of the first reactions after such a tragedy is call for new gun control laws, such as a new assault weapons ban, expanded background checks to close the "gun show loophole," or raising the age at which a person

In early 2018 the Trump administration proposed allowing training certain teachers and staff to carry guns in school buildings, as a way to deter school shooters. The Gallup Organization found that 73 percent of US school teachers opposed this idea, with 58 percent saying that such a proposal would make schools less safe.

can purchase a firearm. However, none of these proposals would have stopped the Santa Fe shooter. Pagourtzis did not use an AR-15 or semiautomatic rifle to kill his victims. Instead, he used a shotgun and a .38 caliber revolver—among the most common firearms available in the United States. Both guns were legally owned by Pagourtzis's father.

Ideally, Pagourtzis's father would have properly secured his firearms in a gun safe, so that his son could not access them. But even that is no guarantee that a massacre couldn't have happened. After all, Pagourtzis also brought several homemade bombs to school with him. Thankfully, they were not detonated—but police later determined that several of the devices were functional.

Setting off such bombs in a school could have resulted in just as many casualties, if not more.

The current laws that regulate the ownership and use of firearms are intended to safeguard the Second Amendment rights of Americans, while also keeping guns out of the hands of those who would misuse them. These laws work, when they are properly enforced.

If Congress were to ban semi-automatic rifles like the AR-15, that might make some people feel safer. But would that make a difference? After all, these weapons account for just a small fraction of the more than 30,000 gun-related deaths each year. Declaring support for tighter background checks draws cheers from the anti-gun crowd, but would do nothing to cut down on the 350 million guns already in circulation in the United States.

Preventing mass shootings requires understanding why

they happen. And unfortunately, a likely reason for the rise in mass shootings in the United States is not something that stricter laws or other measures can adequately address. In a 2015 *New Yorker* essay, journalist and best-selling author Malcolm Gladwell compared the rise of mass shootings to a sort of slow-moving riot. Gladwell referred to a **model** of trends developed by an influential Stanford sociologist, Mark Granovette, who proposed that riots, like other trends, are social processes. Within a riot, people react to the things that others are doing and decide whether to join in.

According to Granovette, riots are started by instigators—those who are ready to throw the first rock through a store window at the slightest provocation. However, most people are not instigators. Instead, they fall somewhere on a spectrum of social behavior. People at the lower end of this spectrum may not be willing to throw the first rock, but they will quickly join in the violence or looting once they see a few other people doing it. Those at the higher end of the spectrum will need to see a larger number of the people around them engaging in the riot before they also set aside their beliefs and join in the riot behavior. Granovette noted that the instigators and those at the lowest level of this spectrum often have strongly held—and sometimes justified—beliefs that they are subject to injustice or persecution. As higher-threshold people join the riot, however, they are less likely to have the same strong feelings that they are the victims of injustice. In other words, they are more "normal" than "angry."

Gladwell proposed that the April 1999 Columbine

shooting was the key event—the "rock through the window"—that started the mass shooting trend. Many subsequent school shooters have copied the methods of the Columbine killers, Eric Harris and Dylan Klebold, or referred to them as role models or heroes. According to Gladwell, each mass shooting lowers the threshold for the next attack, and subsequent attackers tend to have lower levels of grievances.

Some school districts employ "resource officers"— police officers who are specially trained to work in schools— to increase the security in their buildings. This officer works at a school in Manhattan.

L. 11:57:20-63 AM 04/20/99

Surveillance video shows Eric Harris (left) and Dylan Klebold in the cafeteria at Columbine High School during their April 20, 1999, shooting spree. The two young men planned their attack carefully, believing that they would become famous by committing a terrible mass murder. Unfortunately, Harris and Klebold succeeded in inspiring subsequent school shooters, who have copied their methods.

Recent shootings seem to bear this out. Before the 1999 Columbine massacre, Harris and Klebold had reportedly been bullied in school, and both appear to have suffered from mental illnesses. These factors led them to seek revenge for injustices—real or imagined—that had been inflicted upon them by the classmates, and inspired them to plan and carry out the shooting. By contrast, the Santa Fe shooter Pagourtzis was a quiet young man who had been on the honor roll student, was involved in sports, and had came from a loving family. He had not exhibited any "red flags" before this incident.

In his essay, written before the Santa Fe shooting, Gladwell explains:

In the day of Eric Harris, we could try to console ourselves with the thought that there was nothing we could do, that no law or intervention or restrictions on guns could make a difference in the face of someone so evil. But the riot has now engulfed the boys who were once content to play with chemistry sets in the basement. The problem is not that there is an endless supply of deeply disturbed young men who are willing to contemplate horrific acts. It's worse. It's that young men no longer need to be deeply disturbed to contemplate horrific acts.[34]

Many writers have noted that in nearly every mass shooting incident, there were warning signs that were ignored. Rizwan Farook and Tashfeen Malik, who killed fourteen people in San Bernardino, California, in December 2015, had planned their attack for more than a year. Their neighbor later reported that she had seen suspicious activity at their home, but was afraid to report what she saw. On two separate occasions, the FBI investigated Omar Mateen, who claimed to be affiliated with Islamist terrorist groups. Yet those investigations did not raise a red flag when Mateen went into a gun store in Port St. Lucie, Florida. Mateen passed a background check, purchased a handgun and a semi-automatic rifle, and then used those firearms to kill forty-nine people at a gay nightclub in Orlando.

Nearly all mass shooters previously displayed aggressive behavior, mental health issues, or a disturbing fascination with previous killers like the Columbine shooters. Americans need to be aware that these are not "just a phase," but may be warning signs for potential gun violence, and tell authorities any time they see something suspicious.

"We've trained ourselves to mind our own business, to delegate interventions to professionals, and to "judge not" the actions of others. But in a real way, we are our brother's keeper; and an ethic of "see something, say something" is a vital part of community life," writes David French in National Review. "Instead, we all too often retreat into our lives — either afraid that intervention carries risks or falsely comforted by the belief that surely someone else will do the right thing. We've seen this dynamic in other crimes. The worst of the sexual predators revealed (so far) by the #MeToo movement, Harvey Weinstein and Larry Nassar, could have been stopped so much earlier if the people around them had shown just an ounce more courage in the face of *known* complaints and known misconduct. We didn't need better laws to stop rape. We needed better people."[35]

SEEKING
INFORMATION
Pulse Nightclub Shooting
Orlando, Florida
OMAR MIR SEDDIQUE MATEEN - DECEASED

DETAILS
Omar Mir Seddique Mateen, deceased, is believed to be responsible for the shootings at the Pulse nightclub in Orlando, Florida, in the early morning hours of June 12, 2016. The FBI is asking for the public's assistance with any information regarding Mateen.

Even though he had been investigated by the FBI for alleged links to terrorist groups, Omar Mateen passed a background check and was able to purchase firearms. He used those weapons to commit mass murder in Orlando, Florida, in December 2015.

TEXT-DEPENDENT QUESTIONS

1. What was the purpose of the March for Our Lives in March 2018?
2. According to Louis Klarevas, how many gun massacres occurred between 2004 and 2014?
3. Why was the 2018 Santa Fe High School shooting unlike many other recent school shootings?

 ## RESEARCH PROJECTS

Read the report "Implications for the Prevention of School Attacks in the United States," produced by the US Secret Service and the US Department of Education after the Columbine school shooting. (The report is available at: https://www2.ed.gov/admins/lead/safety/preventingattacksreport.pdf.) What are the report's conclusions? Has your school district taken any of the measures suggested to protect students? Write a two-page paper.

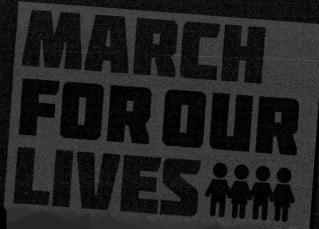

WORDS TO UNDERSTAND

antagonist—a person who actively opposes or is hostile to someone else; an adversary.

appraisal—an active assessment of a person or a situation.

control group—in a scientific study, this is a group of participants that is used as a benchmark by which the response or performance of other participants can be measured.

IS OPEN CARRY IN PUBLIC A PROBLEM?

CHAPTER 4

In recent years, some gun-rights advocates have supported a practice known as "open carry," in which gun owners carry their firearms openly in public. Advocates of this practice believe that a firearm worn in plain sight shows that the gun owner is law-abiding, because criminals often prefer to hide their weapons. Advocates also believe that open carry deters crime, because they believe a criminal will be less likely to attack if there is a "good guy with a gun" in the area.

Opponents of the practice believe that open carry increases the likelihood that everyday disagreements in public places will escalate into deadly conflicts. They say that innocent bystanders may be put at risk by inexperienced or careless gun owners, particularly in states where no license or firearms training is required for open carry. Many people become alarmed or upset to see an armed civilian walking around a shopping mall or a public park. If a concerned bystander calls the police, they are diverting law enforcement officers from other matters, and in the worst case a deadly confrontation could ensue.

Federal law does not restrict open carry, although there are some rules about when firearms may be carried on federal property. Five states—California, Florida, Illinois, New York, and South Carolina—as well as the District of

Columbia have laws banning open carry for handguns. The other forty-five states technically allow the practice of open carry, but several of them do impose restrictions on the open carry of certain types of firearms. The requirements vary in toughness from state to state. And even states that permit open carry still prohibit firearms in certain locations, such as schools, government offices, places where alcohol is served, and on public transportation.

 ## THE ISSUE OF RECIPROCITY

Today, there are a variety of reciprocity agreements—arrangements in which a state agrees to recognize a firearms-related concealed carry (CCW) permit issued by another state. This could include a concealed-carry permit, as well as the legal right to simply travel into the state with a handgun or long gun. Since 2009, several pieces of legislation have been introduced in Congress that would require any valid concealed-carry permit to be recognized anywhere in the country. After the US House of Representatives passed the Concealed Carry Reciprocity Act of 2017, a statement released by the National Rifle Association noted that, "Violent crime and criminals who recognize no restrictions on their own actions are the very reason law-abiding people wish to have their own means of self-protection. Concealed carry reciprocity simply helps even the playing field between law-abiding Americans and predatory criminals." [37]

The essays that follow examine both sides of this question.

OPEN CARRY SHOULD BE BANNED

Opponents of the practice of open carry have several reasons for arguing that it should be banned. Many contend that the mere presence of firearms in public places makes it more likely that people will act aggressively. Over the past five decades there have been more than fifty scientific studies that have indicated this phenomenon,

A famous scientific study found that simply being in close proximity to firearms could increase aggression levels.

> "In a study published in the "Journal of Criminal Law and Criminology", researchers Gary Kleck and Marc Gertz found that of the nearly 2.5 million defensive uses of firearms each year, 92 percent of them scare off their attackers by merely brandishing their firearm. . . . Open carry has been proven to deter crime, which is why we believe it is so important."[36]
>
> —CJ Grisham,
> founder of Open Carry Texas

called the "weapons effect,"[38] does exist.

The first of these studies was conducted in 1967 by Leonard Berkowitz and Anthony LePage. They arranged for study participants to engage with an antagonist who did something to anger or annoy them. (Participants in the study believed the antagonist was, like them, an independent participant, but the antagonist was acting at the direction of the two psychologists.) Later, the participants were brought into a room and asked to decide what level of electric shocks they would give to punish the antagonist. On a table in the room were some items that the researchers explained had been left behind from a previous experiment and not put away. In most cases, the objects included a shotgun and a revolver; in a **control group**, the weapons were replaced with badminton racquets and other sports equipment. Berkowitz and LePage found that participants who were in the room with the guns selected higher levels of electric shock than the control group, signifying a greater level of aggression. More than fifty other experiments since then have duplicated the results, according to *Psychology Today*.

Higher levels of aggression paired with access to guns is more likely to result in a more dangerous society—not a safer one, as pro-gun advocates claim. "Weapons increase all of those aggressive thoughts, feelings, hostile **appraisals** and the type of thinking that somebody's out to get you, or wants to hurt you," notes Ohio State psychology professor Brad Bushman.[39]

Another aspect of this is that when unarmed civilians see a person in public with a gun, they often call the police—even if that armed person is not doing anything illegal. When the police arrive, they must make a quick decision about whether the armed person poses a threat. This can require having to stop and question the armed person, which can result in a tense encounter that is unpleasant at best for all involved.

For a discussion about whether gun control proposals will reduce violence, scan here.

0:00 | 0:00

Sometimes encounters between police and armed civilians can inadvertently turn deadly. In July 2016, a black man named Philando Castile was pulled over by police in Minnesota. During the traffic stop, Castile advised the officer, a white female, that he had a legal permit to carry a firearm and was armed. The police officer warned Castile several times not to reach for his weapon. She then shot Castile when he continued to reach for his pocket. Castile died twenty minutes later. According to Castile's girlfriend, a passenger in the car, Castile had been trying to pull out his driver's license, not his handgun, when he was shot. However, a Minnesota jury subsequently acquitted the police officer of wrongdoing in the shooting.

Signs at a Washington, DC, rally demand justice
for Philando Castile, a black gun owner who was shot and killed
by a Minnesota police officer at a traffic stop.

Some opponents of open carry fear that criminals will attempt to steal firearms if they see them in public.

Open carry advocates often claim that the presence of armed civilians will deter criminals from committing crime. They cite a 1997 study by John Lott and David Mustard, which reported that violent crime rates had fallen between 1977 and 1992 in ten states that had adopted "right to carry" laws. However, subsequent analysis of the data indicated that the effect found by Lott and Mustard may have been due more to the period that was sampled, rather than to an actual effect of the laws. In a 2003 paper scholars Ian Ayers and John J. Donohue found that a similar analysis of violent crime rates from 1991 to 1999 actually indicated an increase in crime in the ten "right to carry" states.[40]

Some advocates believe that wearing guns in public may actually attract criminals, who want to steal the weapons and use them. A 2013 study by Johns Hopkins University found that 10 percent of American police who were killed in the line of duty had been shot with their own guns. Police are highly trained, and secure their firearms in holsters that make it nearly impossible for another person to draw the weapon. If criminals are not deterred by highly trained police officers, they are not likely to be concerned by an armed civilian who would in theory pose much less of a challenge. "Open carry is unsafe, intimidating, and potentially dangerous," wrote Oklahoma State Senator Constance Johnson in an editorial published in *US News and World Report*. "Many first-time 'toters' will also be untrained in retaining control of their own weapons and may make it possible for others to grab their guns and use them against innocent bystanders."[41]

"The safety of our children and families in our communities is paramount, and open carry is not a step in the right direction. We refuse to have to consider whether people who are open carrying around our children and families are members of law enforcement sworn to protect us, or if they are activists making a political statement, or dangerous criminals we should run from."

—Shannon Watts,
founder of Moms Demand Action
for Gun Sense in America

OPEN CARRY SHOULD BE PERMITTED

Americans have always had the right to openly carry a firearm for self-defense, under the Second Amendment. This right was reinforced by the US Supreme Court in 2008, when it ruled in *District of Columbia v. Heller* that a ban on handguns was unconstitutional. According to *Heller* and subsequent cases in federal and state courts, the Second Amendment guarantees Americans the right to bear arms openly outside their home.

Some people become concerned when they notice a civilian walking through a public area with a holstered firearm. They shouldn't be: statistically speaking, a person who is openly carrying a handgun for self-defense is highly unlikely to be involved in criminal activities. A series of studies conducted by the US Department of Justice between 1992 and 2006 concluded that criminals who engaged in armed confrontations with police hid their firearms carefully, and did not carry them openly in a holster. "Most offenders carried firearms in the waistband area without use of a holster for maximum concealment and accessibility," noted the 2006 report *Violent Encounters*.[42]

American economist and gun-rights advocate John Lott studied crime data from states that had passed "right to carry" laws in the United States over a twenty-nine-year period between 1977 and 2005. He found that in states that allowed gun owners to carry firearms openly, violent crime rates declined. In his book *More Guns, Less Crime* (2010), Lott concluded that the decline in violent crime occurs because criminals are deterred from attacking armed civilians. "By now," Lott wrote, "dozens of academics have published studies on right-to-carry laws using national data. These studies have either confirmed the beneficial link between gun ownership and crime or at least not found any indication that ownership increases crime. . . . Not a single referenced study finds the opposite result, that right-to-carry laws have a bad effect on crime."[43]

One report, funded by the Centers for Disease Control during the Obama administration and conducted by the Institute of Medicine and National Research Council, found that Americans regularly use their firearms for self-defense, with estimates of annual use ranging from 500,000 to more than 3 million a year. The study also concluded that firearms are effective tools for self-defense. "Studies that directly assessed the effect of actual defensive uses of guns (i.e., incidents in which a gun was 'used' by the crime victim in the sense of attacking or threatening an offender) have found consistently lower injury rates among gun-using crime victims compared with victims who used other self-protective strategies," the report noted.[44]

Law enforcement officers recognize that most criminals are looking to make a profit, not to get into a gunfight. Criminals tend to avoid places frequented by police officers, and they're unlikely to try to hold up the local gun store during business hours. They'd rather find a place where they feel they have the upper hand. "Obviously there are always the odd exceptions, but clearly, the vast majority of the time a criminal will avoid a deadly

Visitors to Cleveland wear their firearms openly in a public square. Advocates of open carry argue that they have a constitutional right to bear arms openly outside of their homes, and that this practice deters crime.

Several studies have concluded that firearms are an effective form of self-defense, whether in the home or in a public place.

confrontation if they can," notes blogger Dan Zimmerman. "We all know that predators target gun-free zones. When everyone conceals, every zone is gun-free until proven otherwise. With open carry everywhere you go becomes a known 'We have guns!' area."[45]

Rather than seeking to restrict law-abiding Americans from carrying firearms for self-defense, legislators should be looking to make it easier for Americans to defend themselves from those who would do them harm.

TEXT-DEPENDENT QUESTIONS

1. How many states restrict the practice of open carry?
2. What happened to Philando Castile in Minnesota?
3. What practice did John Lott conclude led to the decline of violent crime rates?

 ## RESEARCH PROJECTS

Using your school library or the internet, do some additional research on open carry. Write a one-page essay about whether you think that this practice is more or less likely to deter criminal activity. Use data and anecdotes to support your conclusion.

WORDS TO UNDERSTAND

lobby—an orchestrated effort by the representatives of special-interest groups, called lobbyists, to shape public policy in a way that aligns with their particular group's long-term goals.

attack ad—an advertisement with a message that attacks a candidate or political party about a particular issue in order to gain support for that candidate's opponent.

grassroots—the most basic level of an activity or organization, often involving regular voters rather than trained political operatives.

DOES THE "GUN LOBBY" HAVE TOO MUCH INFLUENCE?

CHAPTER 5

Firearm ownership and gun control are contentious topics in American politics, and polls show that Americans are divided almost equally on the question of whether it is more important to support gun control or to support Second Amendment rights. A Pew Research Center poll from April 2017 found that 51 percent of Americans support gun control, while 47 percent felt it was more important to protect the right of Americans to own guns. A similar poll that Pew took the previous year had nearly the opposite result: 52 percent supported protecting gun owners' rights, while 46 percent backed gun control.[48]

Special-interest groups have formed on both sides of this debate to make sure that their perspectives and policy goals are represented in American politics. Organizations like the National Rifle Association or Gun Owners of America support a broad interpretation of the Second Amendment right to firearm ownership. Other special-interest groups, like the Brady Campaign to Stop Gun Violence or the Coalition to Prevent Gun Violence, push for new laws and restrictions on gun ownership. All of these groups are well funded and highly active. They raise money, run ads that promote their point of view, and mobilize voters in elections. They file lawsuits to achieve their goals through litigation. And they **lobby** political leaders in an effort to influence government policies.

The right to form interest groups and to lobby the government is guaranteed under the First Amendment to the US Constitution, which states that "Congress shall make no law abridging the freedom of speech or of the press, or the right of the people to peaceably assemble, and to petition the government for a redress of grievances."[49] For many Americans, joining a special-interest group is an important way to participate in the political process.

THE NATIONAL RIFLE ASSOCIATION

Today, the National Rifle Association (NRA) is the best-known organization that advocates for the rights of gun owners in the United States. The NRA was founded in 1871 by two former soldiers, William Church and George Wingate. During the Civil War, they had been unimpressed by the marksmanship of many Union soldiers. The organization's original purpose was to improve the shooting skills of American men to prepare them for military service. The NRA organized shooting competitions and encouraged the formation of gun clubs. Among the presidents of the NRA during the late nineteenth century were former Union

generals Ulysses S. Grant, Ambrose Burnside, and Philip Sheridan.

For most of the twentieth century, the NRA was an organization for hunters and sports shooters. From the 1930s to the 1960s, most NRA members were hunters or sportsmen, and the organization often supported state and federal laws that regulated the possession of firearms. But by the late 1960s, the NRA's membership was changing from sportsmen to those who owned handguns for self-protection. After passage of the Gun Control Act of 1968, the NRA's membership grew more opposed to gun control measures.

In 1975, the NRA established a lobbying arm called the Institute for Legislative Action. In 1977, the NRA's bylaws were changed to make defending Second Amendment rights the organization's focus. Since then the NRA has lobbied for gun laws consistent with the broadest possible interpretation of the Second Amendment. "ILA is committed to preserving the right of all law-abiding individuals to purchase, possess and use firearms for legitimate purposes as guaranteed by the Second Amendment to the US Constitution," notes the NRA-ILA web page. "When restrictive "gun control" legislation is proposed at the local, state or federal level, NRA members and supporters are alerted and respond with individual letters, faxes, e-mails and calls to their elected representatives to make their views known."[50]

As of 2018, the NRA had an estimated 5 million members.

Pro-gun advocates rally in Los Angeles, 2018.

The NRA and other groups that support Second Amendment rights are often referred to in the media as the "Gun Lobby." These groups advocate for the rights of gun owners and oppose most, if not all, laws that would restrict or control gun ownership. Representatives of gun-control groups often contend that the Gun Lobby has too much influence over American politics. The short essays that follow will examine both sides of this question.

THE GUN LOBBY HAS TOO MUCH INFLUENCE

The National Rifle Association and other gun-rights organizations have succeeded in blocking any new gun control legislation, largely because of the power they have over lawmakers in Congress as well as in state legislatures. The Gun Lobby spends millions of dollars each year to influence elections—far more than gun-control groups do.

In February 2018, the Center for Responsive Politics reported that gun-rights groups had contributed nearly $13 million to the campaigns of lawmakers currently serving in Congress. By comparison, contributions from gun-control groups to current members of Congress were less than $600,000.

"When the National Rifle Association talks, large swaths of Capitol Hill listen," notes Aaron Kessler in a CNN political report. "The sheer breadth of campaign support provided by the NRA alone over the years helps explain just how deeply the organization is engrained in the election universe. Among the 535 current members of Congress in both the House and the Senate, 307 have received either direct campaign contributions from the NRA and its affiliates or benefited from independent NRA spending like advertising supporting their campaigns."[51]

The NRA and other groups don't only donate their funds to lawmakers, they also actively oppose candidates that are perceived as anti-gun. In 2010, the US Supreme Court ruling in *Citizens United v. the Federal Election Commission* overturned many laws related to campaign

"The National Rifle Association and other gun-rights organizations spent nearly $55 million in the 2016 election cycle to oppose or support candidates through independent spending — nearly 19 times the amount spent by groups promoting gun restrictions, according to a tally by the nonpartisan Center for Responsive Politics."[46]

— journalist Fredreka Schouten

Participants in the March for Our Lives in Washington, DC, hold signs protesting against the influence of the National Rifle Association in American politics.

financing. The *Citizens United* ruling allows special-interest groups like the Gun Lobby to pay for advertising campaigns that attack candidates on specific issues, as long as those campaigns are independent from the opposing political campaign. In other words, these **attack ads** cannot be managed or overseen by the candidate on whose behalf they are attacking. In the 2016 election cycle, the NRA spent more than $50 million on these "independent expenditures." It spent $14.4 million supporting forty-four pro-gun candidates who won, and $34.4 million opposing nineteen anti-gun candidates who lost. These effective campaigns enable the NRA to mobilize gun-rights supporters, who turn out and vote against gun-control

> *"John Locke described the right of self-defense as a 'fundamental law of nature.' It is an unalienable right every bit as essential to human liberty as the right to speak. Indeed, when a person experiences an actual threat, the need to exercise that right of self-defense becomes more immediately primal and deeply felt than any other constitutional right. You can't speak when you're dead. It's hard to practice your religion when you're in the ICU."[47]*

—*journalist David French*

candidates in elections and encourage their like-minded friends to do the same.

"[The Gun Lobby has] a very powerful ability to mobilize a grassroots support and to engage in politics when most Americans can barely be bothered to vote," explains Robert Spitzer, a professor of crime, law and policy and gun control at the State University of New York at Cortland and the author of five books on guns. "I mean more than voting. I mean going to a meeting, writing a letter, contacting a friend. And because so few Americans do those things, if you get a bunch of people in a locality who are all prepared to go out to a meeting they can have a big effect."[52]

THE GUN LOBBY DOESN'T HAVE UNDUE INFLUENCE

Every time there is a mass shooting, the media and gun-control advocates invariably blame the National Rifle Association. They claim that heavy spending by the Gun Lobby prevents politicians from enacting gun control laws that, they believe, would prevent such tragedies from occurring. If only groups like the NRA were not involved in politics, these liberal-leaning organizations seem to think, then everyone could agree on "common sense gun control laws."

However, this is a huge oversimplification of the way that money from special-interest groups influences the political system. There is no doubt that spending by the Gun Lobby does exert an influence on Washington, D.C.—but its advertisements and campaign contributions are far from the only thing that inhibits the passage of new legislation.

In fact, most experts who study the political system recognize that many other special-interest groups spend much more each year on political lobbying than the NRA and other gun-rights groups. The Center for Responsive Politics tracks spending by lobbyists and special interest groups at the website OpenSecrets.org. The National Rifle Association and other gun rights groups do not appear in OpenSecret's list of the top twenty spenders on lobbying efforts. Over the period from 1998 to 2018, that list is headed by the US Chamber of Commerce (over $1.4 billion), the National Association of Realtors ($483 million), and the American Medical Association ($379 million).[53] The total

Republican Senator Ted Cruz of Texas is one of the leading recipients of donations from the gun lobby. During his campaign for the Republican Party's presidential nomination in 2016, he received over $360,000 in donations from gun groups.

from the Gun Lobby lags far behind at an estimated $200 million.

OpenSecrets also tracks spending by industry, breaking it down into 121 categories. The top spenders over the past twenty years include the pharmaceutical, insurance, energy (electric, oil, and gas), and electronics. Spending on lobbying efforts by gun manufacturers is so low it does not even qualify as a separate industry, and is lumped into a miscellaneous category.

Florida Senator Marco Rubio is one American politician who is often linked in the media with the NRA and other groups that defend the Second Amendment. After the

February 2018 school shooting in Parkland, Florida, Rubio was widely criticized in the media because he has accepted roughly $3.3 million from the National Rifle Association since his political career began in 2009. However, while that $3.3 million figure is large, it must be placed in context. Since 2009, Rubio has raised over $91 million in campaign donations, so the NRA's donations represent less than 4 percent of his total. And the NRA or other gun-rights groups are not among the top twenty donors to Rubio's campaign, according to the Center for Responsive Politics.

Rubio himself has expressed what most experts believe is the the real reason that gun-control legislation often fails to pass: many American voters are opposed to it. "The influence of these groups comes not from money,"

Scan here to see a former US soldier respond to some common arguments for gun control.

FOX NEWS channel ▶ RYAN CLECKNER | FORMER SPECIAL OPERATIONS SNIPER
FORMER SNIPER 'DEBUNKS' GUN CONTROL ARGUMENTS

0:00|0:00

US Congresswoman Gabrielle Giffords was badly wounded in a 2011 mass shooting in Tucson, Arizona, that left six people dead and seventeen others injured. After recovering from her injuries, she founded the Giffords Law Center to Prevent Gun Violence, which works with lawmakers to craft gun-control legislation.

the senator told the audience at a town hall meeting televised on CNN shortly after the Parkland shooting. "The influence comes from the millions of people that agree with the agenda, the millions of Americans that support the NRA."[54]

Estimates of the NRA's membership vary from 3 to 5 million people. This is less than 20 percent of American gun owners. But the number of people who tell pollsters that they are NRA members is considerably higher—possibly four times the actual membership. These gun-owning voters are energized and angry about the possibility that government might take their firearms or restrict their Second Amendment rights. They are determined to cast votes for those who they feel are on their side on this issue. They post on Facebook, show up at protests, and donate to candidates and organizations that they believe feel the same way.

If money spent by special-interest groups is enough to "buy" legislation, then gun-control organizations have the same opportunity that gun-rights groups do. Billionaire Michael Bloomberg formed Everytown for Gun Safety in 2014, with the goal of matching the political spending of the Gun Lobby. He promised to spend $50 million on the endeavor—roughly two-and-a-half times the amount that the NRA spends annually. This, you would think, would equalize the playing field.

After the Parkland shooting, Florida Senator Marco Rubio was criticized for accepting contributions from the gun lobby.

In a way, this was reflected in the 2016 presidential election campaign. The media widely publicized the fact that the Republican Party's candidate, Donald Trump, received much more money from gun-rights groups than the Democratic Party's candidate, Hillary Clinton did. OpenSecrets reports that Trump's campaign received $969,138 in donations from pro-gun groups, compared to $48,013 donated by the groups to Clinton. However, what is less-commonly mentioned in media reports is that Clinton's total donations from special-interest groups related to firearms issues were far greater than Trump's. Gun-control advocacy groups such as Everytown for Gun Safety, the Giffords Law Center to Prevent Gun Violence, and the Brady Campaign donated more than $1.1 million to Clinton's campaign, while donating less than $2,000 to the Trump campaign.[55]

Of course the NRA and other organizations that defend Second Amendment rights spend money to promote their ideals and message. That's what all special-interest groups do—and that is their right under the current laws related to spending on political campaigns. But the evidence indicates that the Gun Lobby's success is merely a reflection of the strong feelings of millions of American voters, and each dollar that it spends is no more influential than the dollars spent by other special-interest groups.

TEXT-DEPENDENT QUESTIONS

1. What amendment to the US Constitution allows Americans to form interest groups and lobby the government?

2. How many of the 535 current US congressmen have received donations from the National Rifle Association or support from similar organizations?

3. Who founded Everytown for Gun Safety? What was the founder's goal for this organization?

 RESEARCH PROJECTS

Read the report "Implications for the Prevention of School Attacks in the United States," produced by the US Secret Service and the US Department of Education after the Columbine school shooting. (The report is available at: https://www2.ed.gov/admins/lead/safety/preventingattacksreport.pdf.) What are the report's conclusions? Has your school district taken any of the measures suggested to protect students? Write a two-page paper.

THE FINAL REPORT AND FINDINGS OF THE SAFE SCHOOL INITIATIVE:

IMPLICATIONS FOR THE PREVENTION OF SCHOOL ATTACKS IN THE UNITED STATES

UNITED STATES SECRET SERVICE AND UNITED STATES DEPARTMENT OF EDUCATION

WASHINGTON, D.C.
July 2004

SERIES GLOSSARY OF KEY TERMS

affidavit—a sworn statement, in writing, that sets out a person's testimony.

affirmative action programs—programs that are intended to improve the educational or employment opportunities of members of minority groups and women.

BCE and CE—alternatives to the traditional Western designation of calendar eras, which used the birth of Jesus as a dividing line. BCE stands for "Before the Common Era," and is equivalent to BC ("Before Christ"). Dates labeled CE, or "Common Era," are equivalent to Anno Domini (AD, or "the Year of Our Lord").

colony—a country or region ruled by another country.

democracy—a country in which the people can vote to choose those who govern them.

discrimination—prejudiced outlook, action, or treatment, often in a negative way.

detention center—a place where people claiming asylum and refugee status are held while their case is investigated.

ethnic cleansing—an attempt to rid a country or region of a particular ethnic group. The term was first used to describe the attempt by Serb nationalists to rid Bosnia of Muslims.

felony—a serious crime; in the United States, a felony is any crime for which the punishment is more than one year in prison or the death penalty.

fundamentalist—beliefs based on a strict biblical or scriptural interpretation of religious law.

median—In statistics, the number that falls in the center of a group, meaning half the numbers are higher than the number and half are lower.

minority—a part of a population different from the majority in some characteristics and often subjected to differential treatment.

paranoia—a mental disorder characterized by the strong belief that the person is being unfairly persecuted.

parole—releasing someone sentenced to prison before the full sentence is served, granted for good behavior.

plaintiff—a person making a complaint in a legal case in civil court.

pro bono—a Latin phrase meaning "for the public good," referring to legal work undertaken without payment or at a reduced fee as a public service.

racial profiling—projecting the characteristics of a few people onto the entire population of a group; for example, when police officers stop people on suspicion of criminal activity solely because of their race.

racism—discrimination against a particular group of people based solely on their racial background.

segregation—the separation or isolation of a race, class, or group from others in society. This can include restricting areas in which members of the race, class, or group can live; placing barriers to social interaction; separate educational facilities; or other discriminatory means.

FURTHER READING

Bussard, Michael E. *NRA Firearms Sourcebook: Your Ultimate Guide to Guns, Ballistics, and Shooting.* Fairfax, Va.: National Rifle Association, 2006.

Carter, Gregg Lee, ed. *Guns in American Society: An Encyclopedia of History, Politics, Culture, and the Law.* 2nd ed. Santa Barbara, Calif.: ABC-CLIO, 2012.

Charles, Patrick J. *Armed in America: A History of Gun Rights from Colonial Militias to Concealed Carry.* Amherst, New York: Prometheus Books, 2018.

Jacobs, James B. *Can Gun Control Work?* New York: Oxford University Press, 2002.

Lott, John R. *The War on Guns: Arming Yourself Against Gun Control Lies.* Washington, D.C.: Regnery Publishing, 2016.

Spitzer, Robert J. *Guns Across America: Reconciling Gun Rules and Rights.* New York: Oxford University Press, 2015.

Utter, Glenn H., and Robert J. Spitzer. The Gun Debate: An Encyclopedia of Gun Control and Gun Rights, third ed. Amenia, New York: Grey House Publishing, 2016.

Waldman, Michael. *The Second Amendment: A Biography.* New York: Simon & Schuster, 2016.

Whitney, Craig R. *Living with Guns: A Liberal's Case for the Second Amendment.* New York: Public Affairs, 2012.

Winkler, Adam. *Gunfight: The Battle Over the Right to Bear Arms in America.* New York: W. W. Norton & Co., 2011.

Ziff, John P. *Gun Laws.* Pittsburgh: Eldorado Ink, 2014.

INTERNET RESOURCES

http://www.fbi.gov/about-us/cjis/nics/reports/2012-operations-report
A detailed report from the FBI on the operations of the National Instant
Criminal Background Check System (NICS).

http://www.bradycampaign.org
The Brady Campaign to Prevent Gun Violence advocates for gun control laws.

http://www.nraila.org
The website of the Institute for Legislative Action, the lobbying arm of the
National Rifle Association. This site includes a state-by-state overview of laws
related to firearms ownership.

http://smartgunlaws.org
The California-based Law Center to Prevent Gun Violence provides
information on federal and state firearms laws, analysis of relevant court
decisions, and pro-gun-control policy recommendations.

http://www.handgunlaw.us
This site is regularly updated with information about state and federal statutes
related to firearms ownership.

www.atf.gov
Information on federal and state regulations with regard to firearms ownership
is available on the Bureau of Alcohol, Tobacco, Firearms and Explosives (ATF)
website.

http://www.nrainstructors.org/searchcourse.aspx
This searchable database enables you to find a certified NRA shooting and
safety instructor in your local area.

http://www.boone-crockett.org
Boone and Crockett Club is an organization that promotes wildlife
conservation and hunter safety. It was founded by Theodore Roosevelt in 1887,
making it the oldest such organization in the United States.

http://www.nssf.org/safety
The National Shooting Sports Foundation's web page on firearms safety
includes educational videos and articles about safe and responsible gun
ownership.

CHAPTER NOTES

1 John Stossel, "Gun Control Isn't Crime Control," ABC News (April 26, 2007). https://abcnews.go.com/2020/story?id=3083618&page=1

2 Supreme Court of the United States, "Opinion of the Court: District of Columbia, et al. v. Heller," (October term, 2007), p. 54. https://www.supremecourt.gov/opinions/07pdf/07-290.pdf

4 Bonnie Berkowitz, Denise Lu, and Chris Alcantara. "The Terrible Numbers that Grow with Each Mass Shooting," *Washington Post* (Oct. 1, 2017). https://www.washingtonpost.com/graphics/2018/national/mass-shootings-in-america/

5 US Constitution, amend. II.

6 William Cummings, "For Many Americans, the Second Amendment Is a Defense Against their Own Government," *USA Today* (March 22, 2018). https://www.usatoday.com/story/news/politics/2018/03/22/many-americans-second-amendment-defense-against-their-own-government/379273002/

7 Kim Parker, et al. "The Demographics of Gun Ownership," Social and Demographic Trends, Pew Research Center (June 22, 2017). http://www.pewsocialtrends.org/2017/06/22/the-demographics-of-gun-ownership/

8 Roger B. Taney, quoted in Paul Fink, *Dred Scott v. Sandford: A Brief History with Documents* (Boston: Bedford, 1997), p. 415.

9 Abigail Perkiss, "The Historical Connection between Prohibition, Guns, and Drugs," Constitution Daily (December 21, 2012). https://constitutioncenter.org/blog/the-historical-connection-between-prohibition-guns-and-drugs

10 Supreme Court of the United States, "Opinion of the Court: United States v. Miller, 307 U.S. 174," (1939). https://supreme.justia.com/cases/federal/us/307/174/case.html

11 The National Advisory Commission on Civil Disorders, *The Kerner Report*, intro. by Julian E. Zelizer (Princeton: Princeton University Press, 2016), p. 415.

12 Devin Hughes and Mark Bryant, "We Have All the Data We Need: Stronger Gun Laws Would Save Lives," *Los Angeles Times* (February 26, 2018). http://www.latimes.com/opinion/op-ed/la-oe-hughes-bryant-gun-violence-research-20180226-story.html

13 Eric Pratt, quoted in "Does the US Need Tougher Gun-Control Laws," *Junior Scholastic* (February 20, 2017). https://junior.scholastic.com/issues/2016-17/022017/Does-the-U-S-Need-Tougher-Gun-Control-Laws.html

14 Ellen Nakashima, "FBI: Breakdown in Background Check System Allowed Dylann Roof to Buy Gun," *Washington Post* (July 10, 2015). https://www.washingtonpost.com/world/national-security/fbi-accused-charleston-shooter-should-not-have-been-able-to-buy-gun/2015/07/10/0d09fda0-271f-11e5-b72c-2b7d516e1e0e_story.html?utm_term=.02bb1757e0cd

15 Nakashima, "FBI: Breakdown in Background Check System Allowed Dylann Roof to Buy Gun," *Washington Post.*

CHAPTER NOTES

16 The Gallup Organization, "In Depth: Guns," (accessed June 15, 2018). http://news. gallup.com/poll/1645/guns.aspx

17 Matthew Miller, Lisa Hepburn, and Deborah Azrael, "Firearm Acquisition Without Background Checks: Results of a National Survey," Annals of Internal Medicine 166, no. 4 (January 2017), p. 233-239. http://annals.org/aim/fullarticle/2595892/firearm-acquisition-without-background-checks-results-national-survey

18 Giffords Law Center to Prevent Gun Violence, "Universal Background Checks Fact Sheet," http://lawcenter.giffords.org/gun-laws/policy-areas/background-checks/universal-background-checks/

19 Daniel W. Webster et al., "Preventing the Diversion of Guns to Criminals Through Effective Firearms Sales Laws," Reducing Gun Violence in America (Baltimore: Johns Hopkins Press, 2014), p. 21.

20 104th Congress, Public Law 104-208 (Sept. 30, 1996) 110 Stat. 3009. https://www.gpo.gov/fdsys/pkg/PLAW-104publ208/pdf/PLAW-104publ208.pdf

21 RAND Corporation, "The Effects of Bans on the Sale of Assault Weapons and High-Capacity Magazines," Gun Policy in America. https://www.rand.org/research/gun-policy/analysis/ban-assault-weapons.html

22 Kate Irby, "Nobody Knows Exactly How Many Assault Rifles Exist in the US—By Design," McClatchy DC Bureau (February 23, 2018). http://www.mcclatchydc.com/news/nation-world/national/article201882739.html#storylink=cpy

23 Mark Keefe, "The Truth About Gun Shows," American Rifleman (October 2009). https://www.americanrifleman.org/articles/2016/1/5/the-truth-about-gun-shows/

24 Caroline Wolf Harlow, "Firearm Use by Offenders," Bureau of Justice Statistics Special Report, rev. February 2002. https://www.bjs.gov/index.cfm?ty=pbdetail&iid=940

25 Anthony Fabio, et al. "Gaps Continue in Firearm Surveillance: Evidence from a Large US City Bureau of Police," Social Medicine 10, no. 1 (July 2016), p. 13. http://www.socialmedicine.info/index.php/socialmedicine/issue/view/85

26 Cameron Kasky, quoted in Katie Reilly, "Emma González's Stunning Silence for Parkland: The Latest on March for Our Lives," Time (March 24, 2018). http://time.com/5213929/march-for-our-lives-live-updates

27 Marco Rubio, quoted in Alex Daugherty, "NRA-backed South Florida Lawmakers Say Gun Control Laws Won't Prevent Mass Shootings," Miami Herald (February 15, 2019). http://www.miamiherald.com/news/politics-government/article200395164.html#storylink=cpy

28 Louis Klarevas, Rampage Nation: Securing America from Mass Shootings (Amherst, N.Y.: Prometheus Books, 2016), p. 47.

29 Louis Klarevas, quoted in Christopher Ingraham, "The Real Reason Congress Banned Assault Weapons in 1994—And Why it Worked," Washington Post (February

22, 2018). https://www.washingtonpost.com/news/wonk/wp/2018/02/22/the-real-reason-congress-banned-assault-weapons-in-1994-and-why-it-worked/?utm_term=.39b7663ddd69

[30] Devin Hughes and Mark Bryant, "We Have All the Data We Need: Stronger Gun Laws Would Save Lives," *Los Angeles Times* (February 26, 2018). http://www.latimes.com/opinion/op-ed/la-oe-hughes-bryant-gun-violence-research-20180226-story.html

[31] Jeffrey M. Jones, "US Teachers Prioritize Gun Control to Prevent Shootings," The Gallup Organization (March 22, 2018). http://news.gallup.com/poll/231224/teachers-prioritize-gun-control-prevent-shootings.aspx

[32] Todd Frankel, et al., "Santa Fe School Had a Shooting Plan, Armed Officers, and Practice. And Still 10 People Died," *Washington Post* (May 19, 2018). https://www.denverpost.com/2018/05/19/santa-fe-school-shooting-plan.

[33] Seung-Hui Cho, quoted in John Ziff, *Mass Murderers* (Pittsburgh: Eldorado Ink, 2013), p. 81.

[34] Malcolm Gladwell, "How School Shootings Catch On," *The New Yorker* (October 19, 2015). https://www.newyorker.com/magazine/2015/10/19/thresholds-of-violence

[35] David French, "New Gun Policies Won't Stop Mass Shootings, But People Can," *National Review* (February 15, 2018). https://www.nationalreview.com/2018/02/new-gun-policies-wont-stop-mass-shootings-but-people-can/

[36] CJ Grisham, "A Gun Owner Speaks: My Case for Open Carry," *Daily Beast* (June 12, 2014). https://www.thedailybeast.com/a-gun-owner-speaks-my-case-for-open-carry

[37] National Rifle Association Institute for Legislative Action, "Concealed Carry Reciprocity Passes US House of Representatives," (December 7, 2017). https://www.nraila.org/articles/20171207/concealed-carry-reciprocity-passes-us-house-of-representatives

[38] Leonard Berkowitz and Anthony LePage, "Weapons as Aggression-Eliciting Stimuli," *Journal of Personality and Social Psychology* vol. 7, no. 2 (October 1967), pp. 202–207.

[39] Alan Yuhas, Mere Sight of a Gun Makes Police—and Public—More Aggressive, Experts Say," *The Guardian* (August 5, 2015). https://www.theguardian.com/us-news/2015/aug/05/gun-police-public-more-aggressive-psychology-weapons-effect

[40] Ayres, Ian and Donohue, John J. III, "Shooting Down the More Guns, Less Crime Hypothesis," (2003). Faculty Scholarship Series. Paper 1241. http://digitalcommons.law.yale.edu/fss_papers/1241

[41] Constance N. Johnson, "Open Carry Is an Invitation to Chaos," *US News and World Report* (April 25, 2012). https://www.usnews.com/debate-club/should-people-be-allowed-to-carry-guns-openly/open-carry-is-an-invitation-to-chaos

[42] Anthony Pinizzotto, Edward F. Davis, and Charles E. Miller III, *Violent Encounters: A Study of Felonious Assaults on Our Nation's Law Enforcement Officers*. Washington, D.C.: US Department of Justice, Federal Bureau of Investigation, 2006.

CHAPTER NOTES

43 John R. Lott Jr., *More Guns, Less Crime: Understanding Crime and Gun-Control Laws* (Chicago: University of Chicago Press, 2010), p. vii.

44 Alan I. Leshner et al, eds. *Priorities for Research to Reduce the Threat of Firearm-Related Violence* (Washington, D.C.: The National Academies Press, 2016), p. 16.

45 Dan Zimmerman, "Five reasons Open Carry Is a Good Idea—A Rebuttal," The Truth About Guns (August 21, 2015). http://www.thetruthaboutguns.com/2015/08/daniel-zimmerman/rebuttal-5-reasons-open-carry-is-a-very-good-idea

46 Fredreka Schouten, NRA's Big Spending Pays Off With Clout and Wins in Washington," USA Today (February 15, 2018). https://www.usatoday.com/story/news/politics/2018/02/15/nras-big-spending-pays-off-clout-and-wins-washington/341257002

47 David French, "Why the Left Won't Win the Gun-Control Debate," *National Review* (March 5, 2018). https://www.nationalreview.com/2018/03/gun-control-debate-liberals-wont-win-heres-why

48 Pew Research Center, "Public Views About Guns," June 22, 2017. http://www.people-press.org/2017/06/22/public-views-about-guns/#total

49 US Constitution, amend. I.

50 National Rifle Association-Institute for Legislative Action website (accessed June 14, 2018). https://www.nraila.org/about/

51 Aaron Kessler, "Why the NRA Is So Powerful on Capitol Hill, By the Numbers," CNN.com (February 23, 2018). https://www.cnn.com/2018/02/23/politics/nra-political-money-clout/index.html

52 Robert Spitzer, quoted in Dominic Rushe, "Why Is the National Rifle Association So Powerful?," *The Guardian* (May 4, 2018). https://www.theguardian.com/us-news/2017/nov/17/nra-gun-lobby-gun-control-congress

53 Center for Responsive Politics, "Top Lobbying Firms," https://www.opensecrets.org/lobby/top.php?showYear=a&indexType=l

54 Marco Rubio, quoted in Eli Watkins, "Rubio Stands by Accepting NRA Contributions: People Buy Into My Agenda," CNN.com (February 22, 2018). https://www.cnn.com/2018/02/21/politics/rubio-nra-money-cameron-kasky/index.html

55 Center for Responsive Politics, "Gun Rights vs. Gun Control," OpenSecrets.org. https://www.opensecrets.org/news/issues/guns/

ORGANIZATIONS TO CONTACT

Boone and Crockett Club
250 Station Drive
Missoula, MT 59801
Phone: (406) 542-1888
Fax: (406) 542-0784
Email: bcclub@boone-crockett.org
Website: www.boone-crockett.org

Brady Center to Prevent Gun Violence
1225 Eye Street, NW, Suite 1100
Washington, DC 20005
Phone: (202) 289-7319
Fax: (202) 408-1851
Website:
www.bradycampaign.org

Coalition to Stop Gun Violence
805 15th Street NW, Suite 700
Washington, DC 20005
Phone: (202) 408-0061
Email: csgv@csgv.org
Website: http://csgv.org

Gun Owners of America
8001 Forbes Place, Suite 102
Springfield, VA 22151
Phone: (703) 321-8585
Fax: (703) 321-8408
Website: www.gunowners.org

National Association for Gun Rights
P.O. Box 7002
Fredericksburg, VA 22404
Phone: (877) 405-4570
Fax: (202) 351-0528
Website: www.nationalgunrights.org

National Association of Certified Firearms
Instructors
Tim Grant, President
4722 Forest Circle
Minnetonka, MN 55345
Phone: (952) 935-2414
Email: info@nacfi.us
Website: www.nacfi.us

National Gun Victims Action Council
P.O. Box 10657
Chicago, IL 60610-0657
Email: info@gunvictimsaction.org
Website: http://gunvictimsaction.org

National Rifle Association
11250 Waples Mill Road
Fairfax, VA 22030
Phone: (800) 672-3888
Fax: (703) 267-3989
Website: www.nra.org

National Shooting Sports Foundation
Flintlock Ridge Office Center
11 Mile Hill Road
Newtown, CT 06470
Phone: (203) 426-1320
Fax: (203) 426-1087
Website: www.nssf.org

The Second Amendment Foundation
12500 NE 10th Place
Bellevue, WA 98005
Phone: (425) 454-7012
Fax: (425) 451-3959
Website: www.saf.org
Email: AdminForWeb@saf.org

INDEX

INDEX

AUTHOR'S BIOGRAPHY AND CREDITS

ABOUT THE AUTHOR

Jim Gallagher is the author of more than twenty books for young adults, including *The Johnstown Flood* (Chelsea House), *Causes of the Iraq War* (OTTN Publishing), *Illegal Immigration* (ReferencePoint Press), and *A Girl's/Guy's Guide to Conflict* (Enslow). He lives in central New Jersey with his wife LaNelle and their three children.

PICTURE CREDITS